Pinan Nidan Kata

David Alexander

David Alexander

Caution!

The techniques and theories found within this book are
described solely for reference and have been developed
and obtained over the years through safe training with
professional instructors in a safe environment. The author
and publisher accept **no responsibility** whatsoever that
may result from practicing/performing the techniques and
instructions in this book. Before any change in a fitness
regime one would do well in seeking professional advice.

*Pain is your body saying "stop", please listen to this warning when
training.*

PINAN NIDAN KATA
"PEACEFUL SECOND DEGREE FORM"

Pinan Nidan Kata is sometimes taught before Pinan Shodan Kata as it is deemed simpler in its movements. But traditionally it is the kata for the orange belt grade.

Pinan Nidan kata encompasses techniques that allows one to develop good, simple and effective techniques for self-defence. Blocking techniques are symbolized as striking techniques in parts of the kata for example, head blocks used as forward neck strikes and knife hand strikes in the last two combinations.

The stepping punches in this kata are traditionally targeted at solar plexus height, but the practitioner may adapt to head level punches instead to develop a more effective target for muscle memory.

PINAN NIDAN KATA

1. Facing north, Shoulder width, relaxed stance (yoi)
2. Looking west, turn and shift into a left cat stance and simultaneously perform a left crescent striking block.
3. Advance west into a right stepping punch.
4. Looking over the right shoulder look and turn towards east and shift into a right forward leaning stance and perform a right lower block.
5. Shift backwards slightly into a right cat stance and perform a right crescent striking block.
6. Advance east into a left stepping punch.
7. Looking left towards north, step into a left forward leaning stance and perform a left lower block.
8. Advance north by stepping forwards into a right forward leaning stance and perform a right head block.
9. Advance north by stepping forwards into a left forward leaning stance and perform a left head block.
10. Advance north by stepping forwards into a right forward leaning stance and perform a right head block.
11. Looking over the left shoulder turn and face south-east and shift into a left forward leaning stance and perform a left lower block.
12. Advance south east into a right stepping punch.
13. Looking over the right shoulder turn to face south-west and shift into a right forward leaning stance and perform a right lower block.
14. Advance south west into a left stepping punch.
15. Looking over the left shoulder turn to face south and shift into a left forward leaning stance and perform a left lower block.
16. Advance south by performing a right stepping punch.
17. Advance south by performing a left stepping punch.
18. Advance south by performing a right stepping punch.
19. Looking over the left shoulder shift around and down into a square stance with the torso facing north-east and perform a left lower knife hand block towards north-west

20. Advance forwards north-west stepping through and into a new square stance with the torso facing south-west and perform a right lower knife hand block.
21. Looking over the right shoulder shift around and down into a square stance with the torso facing north-west and perform a right lower knife hand block towards north east
22. Advance forwards north-east stepping through and into a new square stance with the torso facing south-east and perform a left lower knife hand block.
23. Return to "yoi" stance to end the kata.

End of Pinan Nidan kata.

PINAN NIDAN KATA ANALYSIS

Stances:
1. Cat stance
2. Forward leaning stance
3. Square stance

Blocks:
1. Lower block
2. Head block
3. Lower knife hand block/strike

Strikes/Kicks:
1. Crescent strike/block
2. Stepping punch

Pinan Nidan effectively teaches one to defend against the following violent attacks.

- Common hook punches
- Stepping punches
- Kick attacks
- Lapel grabs
- Wrist grabs

BUNKAI

Pinan Nidan Kata interpretation for self-defence:

Techniques 1-6:
An aggressor has thrown a common hook punch towards you (let us assume a right hand punch):

As the opponent attacks with a punch (or anything that involves forward momentum), retreat backwards/diagonally by shifting into a left cat stance to gain distance and avoid attack, simultaneously utilize a left crescent blocking strike to "strike the attack" (it is beneficial to block towards the outside of attack if possible, to potentially make it more difficult for opponent to follow through with yet another attack) then counter with a right stepping punch to the opponent's nose or neck.

Techniques 1-6:
An aggressor has thrown a common hook punch towards you (let us assume a right hand punch):

As the opponent launches an attack avoid and block with the utilization of both hands to perform a right lower block as a strike to the opponents groin (for example block with a left intercepting block and grab the opponent's punch, then pull on the arm whilst snapping the right hand into the groin) then circle the lower block up and around and down to strike the opponent's nose ('Jodan' high level), be sure to drop into a cat stance to develop downwards momentum into this strike then step through into a left punch to the solar plexus or head.

Techniques 1-6:
An aggressor has launched a right front kick at you:
The initial combination found in Pinan Nidan can also be utilized as a defence against a front kick. First avoid by sliding toward the inside of the attack into a left cat stance and aim to strike the opponents thigh area with a left crescent striking block as the kata suggests, then follow through with a right stepping punch driving through the opponent's solar plexus or head

.

Techniques 7-10:
Although there are people who use this basic combination of techniques in its full sequence as a block, strike, grab and throw/lock, this is unrealistic therefore please find here the most basic uses of this kata combination.
An aggressor has launched a right front kick at you:
As a defence against a front kick, first avoid by sliding backwards in a forward leaning stance and block with a left lower block, then when the kick has landed step through and strike the neck with a right high level block to the opponents neck to force the opponent backwards. This interpretation can adapt to be utilized on the outside of the opponent's kick also.

Techniques 7-10:
An aggressor has thrown a common hook punch towards you (let us assume a right hand punch):
Advancing in a forward leaning stance with high level head blocks in this section of Pinan Nidan explains that striding forwards as a defence against a punch/s whilst blocking can gain the karateka an advantage. Therefore as the attack approaches, advance and block with a left head

block, then advance into the opponent with a right head block as a strike to the neck, (this defence can also utilize an initial avoidance motion towards the inside or outside, or even a retreat by stepping back then stride forwards).

Techniques 11-18:
An aggressor has thrown a common hook punch towards you (let us assume a right hand punch):

It may appear that a lower block defends only from attacks to the lower areas, but essentially the definition of "lower block" is describing the motion of applying a downwards force, therefore if one can direct a common hook punch directed towards his/her head downwards it certainly does well to open up the opponent's defence making them vulnerable to a counter attack, this is what Pinan Nidan seems to be explaining to us due to the many lower blocks found within it. Therefore utilizing this section of Pinan Nidan as a defence against a punch/s, as the attack approaches avoid by either sliding or stepping backwards and towards the inside of the punch, and as the punch travels past its target (you) guide the punch down at this point with a left or right lower block correctly utilizing the complete arc of motion block effectively and force the attack down and away, then counter with a swift stepping punch with the opposite hand to the solar plexus or head.

Techniques 11-18:
An aggressor has thrown a common hook punch towards you (let us assume a right hand punch):

To re-illiterate the full use of both hands in the motion of a lower block, one can block the punch with the left arm, then bring the right hand around and grab the opponent's wrist and shift the opponent around so that you are on the outside of their defence, and whilst maintaining the grip with your right, snap your left fist down onto the opponent's elbow to lock/break, then step through into a right stepping punch to the lowered head of the opponent, where the side of the head would be normally exposed if you have lowered their torso due to the elbow lock, therefore a perfect target would be the ear or temple.

Techniques 11-18:
An aggressor has launched a right front kick at you:

As a defence against a front kick, avoid (in any direction) and perform the relevant side lower block then instantly step through into a stepping punch to the head or solar plexus.

Techniques 19-22:
An aggressor has thrown a common hook punch towards you (let us assume a right hand punch):

This section of Pinan Nidan utilizes the power of dropping into a square stance to strike. First block the punch with a left knife hand block and grab, then transfer this grip to the right hand and simultaneously guide the punch to the right and lower into a square stance (now outside of the opponent's attack) and strike the opponent's groin with a left lower knife hand strike.

Techniques 19-22:
An aggressor has launched a right front kick at you:

As the attack is launched step back (outside of the attack) and down into a square stance and block with a right lower knife hand block, then step through into another square stance and strike down into the groin area with a left lower knife hand strike.

SELF-DEFENCE FROM COMMON GRABS AND HOLDS

Techniques 7-10 from Pinan Nidan kata:

An aggressor has approached and gripped your clothing at the lapel with their right arm and has posed their left fist as if to threaten you with a punch:

Assume a good stance (if you are pushed against a wall utilize a cat stance or the hour glass stance), and raise the right arm up and over the outside of the opponent's hold on you as a head level block (this motion alone will help prevent your opponent from utilizing a punch with their free hand). Then circle this over and down onto your opponents arm, then strike your opponent's head with either a punch or another head level block/strike to the opponent's jaw.

Techniques 1-6 from Pinan Nidan

An aggressor has taken hold of your wrist, either with one or both of their hands:

Let's assume the opponent has grabbed/restrained your left arm/wrist using their grip. Utilizing the effect of a quick shift in a left cat stance, simultaneously disable the opponent's grip using the full motion of a left crescent strike, then attack with a right stepping punch to the opponent's nose.

Notes

_____

_____

_____

_____

_____

_____

_____

_____

_____

_____

_____

_____

_____

_____

_____

_____

Notes

Notes

_____

_____

_____

_____

_____

_____

_____

_____

_____

_____

_____

_____

_____

_____

_____

_____

Notes

_____

_____

_____

_____

_____

_____

_____

_____

_____

_____

_____

_____

_____

_____

_____

Notes

_____

_____

_____

_____

_____

_____

_____

_____

_____

_____

_____

_____

_____

_____

_____

_____

Notes

_____

_____

_____

_____

_____

_____

_____

_____

_____

_____

_____

_____

_____

_____

_____

_____

_____

Notes

_____

_____

_____

_____

_____

_____

_____

_____

_____

_____

_____

_____

_____

_____

_____

Notes

_____

_____

_____

_____

_____

_____

_____

_____

_____

_____

_____

_____

_____

_____

_____

_____

ABOUT THE AUTHOR

David Alexander has trained in karate most of his life. He has
published numerous resources on the subject.

Other books available on Amazon:

Karate in Modern day use

Shukokai Karate Kata

This booklet is part of the Shukokai kata booklet series